My Country
Great Britain

Cath Senker

A+
Smart Apple Media

Published by Smart Apple Media,
an imprint of Black Rabbit Books
P.O. Box 3263, Mankato, Minnesota 56002
www.blackrabbitbooks.com

Published by arrangement with the Watts
Publishing Group LTD, London.

Library of Congress Cataloging-in-Publication Data
Senker, Cath. Great Britain / by Cath Senker.
pages cm.—(My country)
Includes bibliographical references and index.
Summary: "Jake, a young boy from Great Britain,
introduces readers to his country's landscape, weather,
foods, and festivals. Jake also tells readers about his
school, family life, and things to see in Great Britain.
Includes a page of facts about Great Britain's population,
geography, and culture"—Provided by publisher.
ISBN 978-1-59920-909-8 (library binding)
1. Great Britain—Juvenile literature. 2. Great Britain—
Social life and customs—Juvenile literature. I. Title.
DA27.5.S46 2015
941—dc23
                2012042904

Series Editor: Paul Rockett
Series Designer: Paul Cherrill for Basement68
Picture Researcher: Diana Morris

Picture credits: Mike Booth/Alamy: 15t; David Burrows/
Shutterstock: 1, 6; Richard Clark/istockphoto: 2, 18; Roger
Cracknell/Alamy: 19; Kathy de Witt/Alamy: 7b; Empics/
PAI: 5; Gemenacom /Shutterstock: front cover cl, 4t, 7bl,
11bl, 15b, 17b, 21b, 22t; Granata1111/Shutterstock: 22b;
David Hughes/Shutterstock: 9; Gail Johnson/Shutterstock:
front cover cr; Liquoricelegs/Dreamstime: 14; Anthony
McAulay/Shutterstock: 8; Ken McKay/Rex Features: front
cover cl; Padmayogini/Shutterstock: 11b, 24; Ina Peters/
istockphoto: 10; rambo182/istockphoto: 4b; Helene Rogers/
Art Directors/Alamy: 13; Samot/Shutterstock: 20; Iain
Sarjeant/istockphoto: 3, 21; Homer Sykes/Alamy: 12;
Janine Wiedel/Alamy: 16; Willsie/istockphoto: 17.

Printed in Stevens Point, Wisconsin at Worzalla
PO 1654
4-2014

9 8 7 6 5 4 3 2 1

Contents

All words in **bold**
appear in the
glossary on page 23.

Great Britain in the World

Hi! My name is Jake, and I come from Great Britain.

Great Britain is an island in Western Europe. A medium-sized country, it is made up of England, Wales, and Scotland.

SCOTLAND

Edinburgh ·

Manchester ·

WALES   ENGLAND

Cardiff ·   · London

Great Britain's place in the world.

Great Britain is one of the world's richest countries.

I live in Manchester, a big, important city in the north of England. We have two famous soccer teams.

A popular soccer team, Manchester United, plays in red and white at their soccer stadium, Old Trafford.

People Who Live in Great Britain

A mix of British people at a London market.

Around 60.5 million people live in Great Britain. People from all over the world have made it their home.

Many come from the Caribbean, India, Pakistan, and other countries.

Most people in Great Britain live in cities. The biggest city is the **capital**, London. It has almost 8 million people!

Nearly half of us live near the **coast**. Some people live in the countryside.

In the countryside, walking and cycling are popular.

My grandparents came to Great Britain from Ireland.

What Great Britain Looks Like

Much of the **landscape** is hilly with low mountains. In the east and southeast, the land is flat. Many beaches are around the long **coastline**.

Scotland has many mountains, and it often snows in winter.

The countryside is covered in farmland. Around one-quarter of the land is used for farming.

Big cities like Manchester are packed with busy roads, homes, shops, and offices. Our cities also have plenty of parks.

East Anglia, in eastern England, is flat and good for growing crops.

At Home with My Family

All kinds of families live
in Great Britain. Many children
live with both parents. Some
live with one parent or have
a stepfamily.

Many families love
playing video games.

We mostly enjoy entertainment at home, such as watching TV and playing on computers.

We also like to get together with grandparents, aunts, uncles, and cousins.

I like going shopping with my family.

What We Eat

In Great Britain, we like to eat meat, potatoes and vegetables, fish and chips, pies, and sandwiches. We are fond of fast food, such as burgers and pizza.

we call fries "chips" and like to eat them with salt and vinegar.

We have food from all over the world! British people enjoy curries, which is an Indian dish.

British people also like sweet foods. We love cakes, cookies, and chocolate.

This family is buying a take-out meal to eat at home.

My favorite treat is chocolate cake. What's yours?

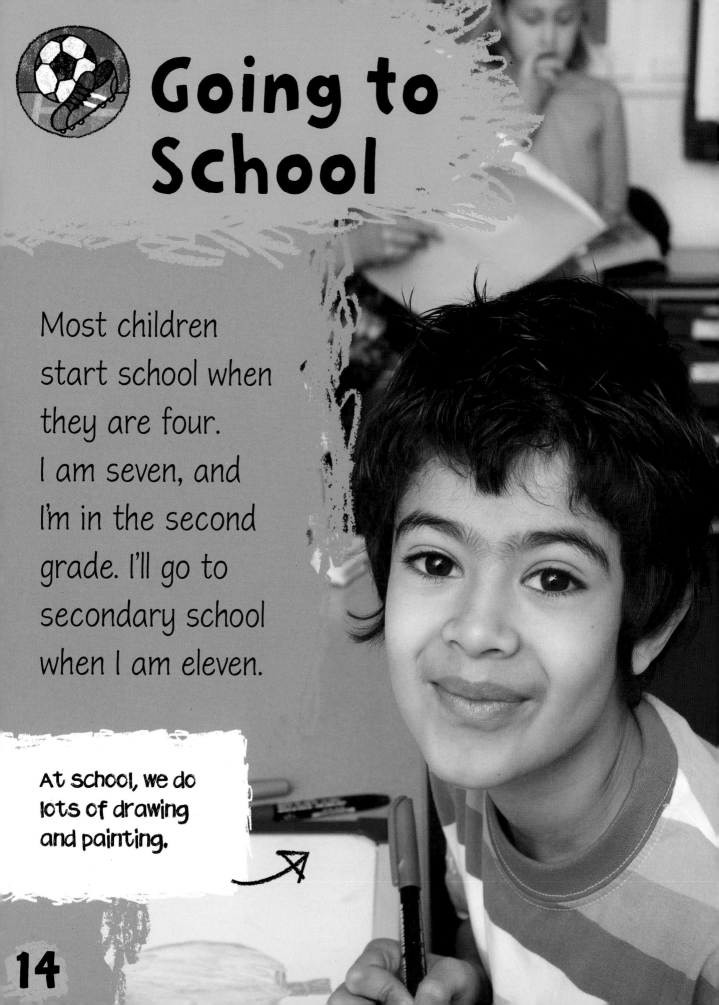

Going to School

Most children start school when they are four.
I am seven, and I'm in the second grade. I'll go to secondary school when I am eleven.

At school, we do lots of drawing and painting.

The school day starts at 9:00 in the morning. We all eat our lunch at school. School ends at 3:00.

Most children eat school lunch, but some bring a packed lunch.

At 3:00, I go to after-school club until my parents finish work and pick me up.

Having Fun

In our free time, we mostly have fun at home. We visit our friends' houses to play. Often, we go to the **local** park.

we love to play on the jungle gyms at the playgrounds.

During school breaks, some people travel to hotter countries to enjoy the sunshine.

Others stay in Great Britain. They may go camping or visit the ocean.

When the sun comes out, people head for the ocean beaches.

I love playing in the sand at the beach. The ocean is very cold!

Holidays and Celebrations

christmas is a christian holiday, but everyone enjoys the special day.

Our main **holiday** is Christmas on December 25. January 1, New Year's Day, is a big holiday too.

In Scotland especially, people celebrate **New Year's Eve** with street parties and music.

On November 5, people light bonfires and fireworks to celebrate **Bonfire Night.**

People of different religions celebrate their own holidays. For example, Muslims hold a delicious feast to celebrate **Eid al-Fitr.**

Firework displays light up the sky on Bonfire Night.

Things to See

Most visitors to Great Britain head to London. The sights include Buckingham Palace and many museums. The London Eye ride offers fantastic views of the city.

On the London Eye, you can see as far as 25 miles (40 km) on a clear day!

Edinburgh, Manchester, Birmingham, and Cardiff have many sights too.

Across the country are zoos, theme parks, and castles. You can climb hills and walk around lakes and forests.

Edinburgh castle in Scotland attracts thousands of visitors each year.

I love visiting castles although they can be creepy.

Here are some facts about my country!

Fast Facts about Great Britain

Capital Cities = London is the capital city of Great Britain and England; Edinburgh is the capital of Scotland; Cardiff is the capital of Wales.

Population = 60.5 million

Area = 89,000 square miles (230,500 km^2)

Languages = English and Welsh

National holiday = Christmas Day

Currency = pound sterling

Main religions = Christianity, Islam, Hinduism

Longest river = River Severn, 220 miles (355 km)

Highest mountain = Ben Nevis, 4,400 feet (1,345 m)

Glossary

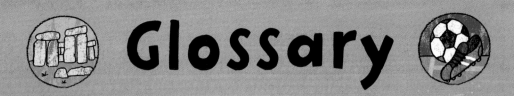

Bonfire Night the festival to remember when Guy Fawkes tried, but failed, to blow up the king and Parliament in 1605

capital the country's seat of government

coast where the land meets the sea

coastline the land along a coast

Eid al-Fitr a three-day Muslim festival to celebrate the end of the holy month of fasting (going without food for religious reasons)

holiday a special time when people celebrate something

landscape what a place looks like

local to do with the place where you live

New Year's Eve the night before New Year

stepfamily the family formed when a parent marries again

Further Information

Websites

www.bbc.co.uk/newsround/

www.projectbritain.com/

Books

Atkinson, Tim. *Discover the United Kingdom (Discover Countries)*. PowerKids Press, 2012.

Burgan, Michael. *United Kingdom in Our World (Countries in Our World)*. Smart Apple Media, 2012.

Simmons, Walter. *England (Exploring Countries)*. Bellwether Media, 2011.

 # Index